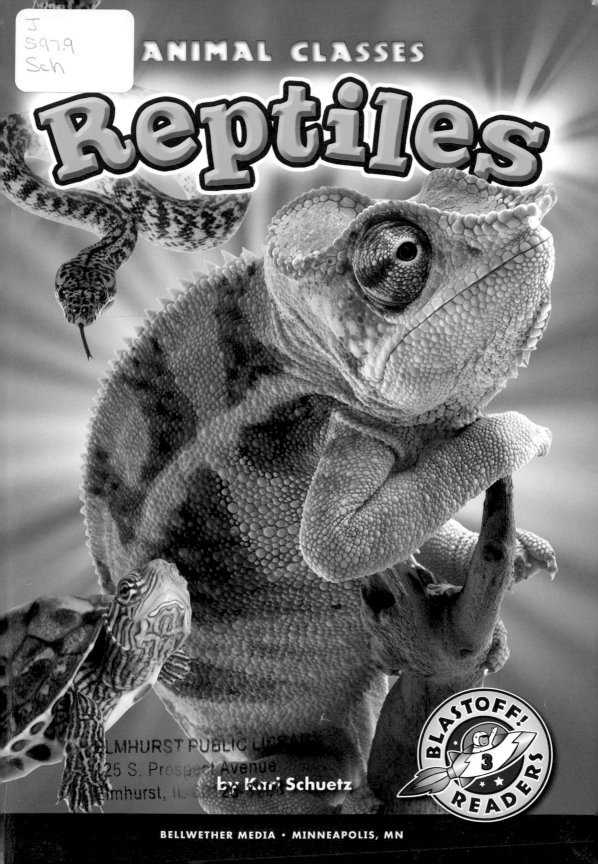

ANIMAL CLASSES

Reptiles

by Kari Schuetz

BELLWETHER MEDIA • MINNEAPOLIS, MN

BLASTOFF!
READERS
3

Note to Librarians, Teachers, and Parents:

Blastoff! Readers are carefully developed by literacy experts and combine standards-based content with developmentally appropriate text.

Level 1 provides the most support through repetition of high-frequency words, light text, predictable sentence patterns, and strong visual support.

Level 2 offers early readers a bit more challenge through varied simple sentences, increased text load, and less repetition of high-frequency words.

Level 3 advances early-fluent readers toward fluency through increased text and concept load, less reliance on visuals, longer sentences, and more literary language.

Level 4 builds reading stamina by providing more text per page, increased use of punctuation, greater variation in sentence patterns, and increasingly challenging vocabulary.

Level 5 encourages children to move from "learning to read" to "reading to learn" by providing even more text, varied writing styles, and less familiar topics.

Whichever book is right for your reader, Blastoff! Readers are the perfect books to build confidence and encourage a love of reading that will last a lifetime!

This edition first published in 2013 by Bellwether Media, Inc.

No part of this publication may be reproduced in whole or in part without written permission of the publisher. For information regarding permission, write to Bellwether Media, Inc., Attention: Permissions Department, 5357 Penn Avenue South, Minneapolis, MN 55419.

Library of Congress Cataloging-in-Publication Data
Schuetz, Kari.
 Reptiles / by Kari Schuetz.
     p. cm. – (Blastoff! readers: animal classes)
 Includes bibliographical references and index.
 Summary: "Simple text and full-color photography introduce beginning readers to reptiles. Developed by literacy experts for students in kindergarten through third grade"–Provided by publisher.
 ISBN 978-1-60014-776-0 (hardcover ; alk. paper)
 1. Reptiles–Juvenile literature. I. Title.
 QL644.2.S337 2013
 597.9–dc23   2011053036

Printed in the United States of America, North Mankato, MN.

Table of Contents

The Animal Kingdom

Large or small, hairy or **scaly**, all animals belong to the animal kingdom.

Members of the animal kingdom
are grouped by common traits.

What Are Reptiles?

Animals with backbones are called **vertebrates**. Reptiles are one of the five main **classes** of vertebrates.

The Animal Kingdom

vertebrates

examples of animals with backbones

- amphibians
- birds
- fish
- mammals
- reptiles

invertebrates

examples of animals without backbones

- arachnids
- crustaceans
- insects

Reptiles are scaly-skinned animals. They **shed** their skin when it gets too old or tight.

They are also **cold-blooded**. Reptiles **bask** in the sun to stay warm and find shade or water to cool off.

Most baby reptiles hatch from eggs. Mothers often lay their eggs in nests or holes.

Some adults stay to guard the eggs, but most do not. Babies are often on their own after they hatch.

tortoise

Reptiles are divided into four main groups. Turtles and tortoises make up one group. Both animals have hard shells.

Turtles spend a lot of time in water. **Webbed feet** help them swim. Tortoises walk at a slow pace on land.

turtle

webbed feet

Lizards and snakes are another main reptile group. These animals crawl on short legs or slither on their bellies.

They stick out their tongues to smell for food. Some, such as the Komodo dragon and king cobra, kill their prey with a **venomous** bite.

Komodo dragon

alligators

Alligators and crocodiles make up another group. These reptiles often **lurk** in or near water.

Strong jaws and sharp teeth make alligators and crocodiles frightening predators.

crocodile

The tuatara is the lone member of the last reptile group. It has spiky scales down its back and tail.

tuatara

Scientists call the tuatara a living **fossil**. Its **extinct** relatives roamed the earth with dinosaurs!

Largest:
saltwater crocodile

Smallest:
dwarf gecko

Longest:
reticulated python

Fastest:
spiny-tailed iguana

Longest Life Span/Slowest:
giant tortoise

Shortest Life Span:
Labord's chameleon

**spiny-tailed
iguana**

reticulated
python

Glossary

bask—to lie in the sun

classes—groups within the animal kingdom; members of a specific class share many of the same characteristics.

cold-blooded—having a body temperature that changes to match the temperature of its surroundings

extinct—no longer existing on Earth

fossil—physical proof of an animal or plant from long ago

lurk—to stay hidden and wait for prey

scaly—covered with hard plates called scales

shed—to let fall off; reptiles shed their skin when it becomes too old or tight.

venomous—able to harm or kill with venom; venom is a poison that some animals produce.

vertebrates—members of the animal kingdom that have backbones

webbed feet—feet with thin skin connecting the toes

To Learn More

AT THE LIBRARY

Arnosky, Jim. *Slither and Crawl: Eye to Eye with Reptiles*. New York, N.Y.: Sterling, 2009.

Berger, Gilda and Melvin. *True or False: Reptiles.* New York, N.Y.: Scholastic, 2008.

Wilson, Hannah. *Life-Size Reptiles*. New York, N.Y.: Sterling, 2007.

ON THE WEB

Learning more about reptiles is as easy as 1, 2, 3.

1. Go to www.factsurfer.com.

2. Enter "reptiles" into the search box.

3. Click the "Surf" button and you will see a list of related Web sites.

With factsurfer.com, finding more information is just a click away.

Index